HALF IN /HALF OUT

Poems by Number 69758

JULIO FERNANDO VELEZ

InspiringVoices®

Inspiring Voices books may be ordered through booksellers or by contacting:

Inspiring Voices
1663 Liberty Drive
Bloomington, IN 47403
www.inspiringvoices.com
1 (866) 697-5313

ISBN: 978-1-4624-1251-8 (sc)
ISBN: 978-1-4624-1252-5 (e)

Library of Congress Control Number: 2019900550

Print information available on the last page.

Inspiring Voices rev. date: 02/19/2019

DEDICATION:

In 1967 we lived in Asheboro, North Carolina. I was about 17 years old, and we were the only Latino family in town. We would go to NYC for major holidays to be with family. Upon returning to school after a holiday, I was supposed to take an English exam in the class of Mrs. Kittie J. Caveness. I was caught writing something on a scrap piece of paper. Mrs. Caveness asked me what little girl I was bothered over. My reply was none. She said, "Then you are cheating on your test. Give me those notes." I did as she asked, and she started to read out loud: "Your homies are pushing...." She stopped and said, "Honey, I am not from a big metropolitan city. Please read this out loud." So I did:

> *Your homies*
> *are pushing*
> *Time,*
> *Dope,*
> *and Daisies.*

She then asked what it meant. I told her that when we go back home to NYC, one or more of my friends are always pushing time (in jail), dope (strung out), or daisies (dead).

She then said that I should write a book about that hell I called home; and maybe, just maybe, some NYC kid will read it in time to walk away from there and come out alive. I didn't have time to write a book then, but two years later as I was kicking cold turkey while standing in the yard of the world's largest prison, I began my story.

My English teacher in North Carolina did what no other teacher had ever done. She reached for me and inspired me to write. I would like to dedicate this book to her.

Dedicated to Kittie Caveness

THANKS:

The author wishes to express his deep gratitude to his children and to their mother.

EDITOR'S NOTE: The content of this book is presented in a somewhat raw form. Spelling and grammar were corrected only when it was necessary for the sake of clarity. Otherwise, the original spelling, capitalization, and punctuation styles were all preserved from the hand-written poems. It is the editor's hope that this will contribute to the authentic, honest tone with which the poet presents his emotions and experiences.

1949–1970

Just like a kid
Using their eyes
And trusting.

As Little Man pulls his dirty sleeve over his redden, tear soaked,
unblinking eyes he asked
"You are going to help me right Tony, right, right Tony"

Tony throws his arm around this little man and pulls him in close
and answered
"Sure I am Little Man, where is this mother fucker"

As Little Man tries his best to stop crying to compose himself to talk,
Tony and this kid, his fellow 3rd grader head into the Bowels of hell
to find that 5th grader that keeps bullying Little Man's younger
brother.
They cross at the intersection of Kelly Street and Intervale Ave
and as if in slow motion they enter the schoolyard at PS 99.
No body messes with us Bro. Nobody messes with The White
Warriors.

Thanks Tony, I knew I could count on you.

I'V NEVER PLAYED WITH MY FATHER
    NEVER JOINED THE SCOUTS NOR THE
    LITTLE LEAGE
    NEVER REALLY HAD ANY FRIENDS AT ALL
        AT THE TENDER AGE OF NINE
    HAD MY BACK TO THE WALL
    NEW YORK CITY BORN AND BRED
    WARM GUN IN MY ARM BRINGS
    COLD GUN TO YOUR HEAD.

I remember walking to the mess hall and the guys whispering as I passed them.

I didn't know what was going on but I as hungry. So I walked in and sat where I always did. With the Briar Cottage. There were 11 cottages here at Lincoln Hall.

You see at an early age I was doing time.

As I start to eat, somebodies big brother… Comes over to me and says. Yo Tony, I heard you took a beating for not dropping a dime? Listen around here a guy who can keep his trap shut, is a stand up guy.

I had just graduated from high school.
It was 1968 and I left home for the second time in my life.
The first was to go to reformatory when I was 12 years old.

I was engaged to a great girl and she lived with her grandmother in the Bronx.
I moved in with my girlfriends mother
    and got a job at Kress 5&10 on Southern Blvd and westchester ave.
It was a blast of a summer and I was having the time of my life
Thats when I walked into a room full of drugs. I ran out and slamed the door behind me
As I leaned up against the door, I realized that it had taken me twenty years to actually leave that room.

They were light and inspiration
In a season of rain

I shine your shoes
With the water I drink

It's the hardest job
Trying to stop children
From killing children
Selling dope
Futures going up in smoke

I just don't know
what to do –
Being I'm so in love with you
Thinking of the times I've put you through
The good and the bad of love filled blues

Going down the highway
    This cloudy day
Knowing I won't see you
    No, I can't stay

I've wrote you a note
    I'll leave behind
Thanking you, and loving you
    For being so kind.

And here I sit
   Amazed
Yet, I had a love,
   Like and used it with no faze.

How much more
do you want from life?

Making me cry
early in the morning
and late at night.

You can't get me
I am cold, calloused and mean.
No one can get beside my wake of deathful bond
No none
Please girl, leave me alone

TURNED 21 ON THE LAM
    RIDING A TRAIN INTO NYC
    DOING AN INTERSTATE FLIGHT
    HID BY DAY RAN BY NIGHT

1970–1975

I've stood in the yard
    Of the worlds largest prison.
Shooting hoops, juggling contraband
Eating some swag.
    Spinning tales, passing out short ice, dealing crates and
conning New York City cons,
as I am better than your best.
  My word is bond, I am the "Go To Guy" if it's there I can get it,
        whatever it is, I can make it happen.
I loan out my smokes and with just your word, you buy it.
Please don't cross me
As I fight like a prison riot

When I walked into the Tombs
I had a call to make to my lawyer
I called my girlfriend instead
Broke her heart and was led into
The house of the dead

This is not the story of pain wherein
    the entire football team rallies behind you as they visit you in
    the hospital
    nor the broken heart that gets a second breath as Sally Sophomore
    throws her arms
        around the one who mistakes abuse for love
    nor the group of people who surround the little boy being
    attacked by a rival gang.
But, I urge you to entertain the warm fuzzy of a not so gentle
    group hug
    as 5 champion demons surround, subdue, and methodically
    inject a plague of depression
    into the lifeless soul of a lost man with no home to call his own.
A Depression 101 graduate
    who first opened his word dictionary at the Ivy League Rikers
    Island U.
    Where his fraternity of broken men, met daily in 8. Block B Side.

No one is looking
       No one is there.
No one is smiling
       No one cares.
I thought it was only movie shit
       But look I am in the slammer
Real bars, tin foil walls
       And men with hands like hammers

Disperse, Disperse, Disperse, Disperse!
As the chickens, horses, cows and sheep
Had all sought his own kind to talk; not meet.
The lambs were told to disperse, and mind you
They did. But no other group was likewise instructed.
And being it was not their home, they followed orders.
They went on to run around and condition their bodies.
For nowhere did it say they could not—but as you
Guessed it, a new rule was added. As a flock they
Could not be taken, for like a solid wall they were.
So they told them all is well or really said nothing
At all. Then as the lambs paired off and went away in
Groups of twos and threes and sometimes one—they
Locked them in the wood shed to turn their views
To those of white sheep for we were all black lambs.
One by one they told us we were wrong, but nowhere
Was there a rule or law to clarify this statement.
So as the true Animal Farm code goes—one was
Made up shortly thereafter and placed as warning to all.

Back behind me swine!
You, of no count dignity.
If not for no one then at least for yourself.
Go about and clear this air.
I've inquired to you two times
              Two too many times
              Both by question
              And by eye.
Yet you go on as a low snake.
Crawling from my vision to
Smirk and hiss
Laughter of blue-eyed smoke.

Man landed on the moon on July 1969
    the same month that I went into orbit.
If loneliness were money
    It is I and I alone that
    has paid the way to the moon
    and back.
October 1972
    second launch made at night/Elmira
    Last mission to the moon
    No one had ever been back

The flower is so, so aware
Of sunlight, rain and frost.
It trembles in the 6 o'clock
Shadow of dusk.
Yet, and all it knows not the unfriendly
Winds of a storming blizzard.
It has always been a calm setting
Of true soils for this flower.

Am I not a beast for even
Thinking of falling on it.
With a fanning of words propelled by need
A need not returned
Showering it in a rain.

Storming Anger, known only by
    Those who have amended today
    To walk tomorrow.

Seek no more.
As I am the way.
Don't turn another foot
In either direction
Let me lead.
Go as I into the night
With but Faith
As my light.

I fumble once on a step
Which squeaks,
Then after I burrow
My hands in my pockets
Knowing no more the rush
Of a soundless night.

Thrust for a sling in my band
Of walled in comfort.
Keep it. For it is of no worth.
No, not lest you turn off
The Light.

Oh flower of mortal delight
    As a bird in solo flight –
I linger on your wings of night
Known only by those
    Who barely see today
    For yesterday is gone
    And tomorrow is to come.

Plan for it
    But live
        For today.

13517

Reach the top of the stairs.
Go beyond
Look no more
As you
Have now become part of your own.

Blow two lines
Of trailing snow
From your path; of illicit recruit.

Salvage together
That which belongs
To neither.
Bring to pass the present
Which wholly belongs
To a breeding mother of
Blues-filled sanity.
Go past
Go beyond
Go, into yourself and see the beauty
You show me day in and day out.

But go now, or never see!

Lifting my head
    Above the clouds
I shift for support
    Only to find the wind
      Way too loud.

Fasten your seat belts
    And smoke no more
    Flashing wistfully,
    I find the door.

     Soaring!
   Soaring!
Soaring!
    On a white snowbound
Airline

Glaringly I stomp my wishes from my heart.
I wish you no harm, so please, in peace let us part.
Go about your TCB's as I go on mine
    Making sure not to cross the line.
I seek my will at all cost
      But not if it means your respect must be at a loss
       I get off where others get on
        Only to touch your heart
         with great alarm.

Don't fear what you see, as you know it not.
But rest assured, I'll try you
    in no way
      or type
        or phase.

For you alone can cause your disgrace.

The truth is non-realistic
On a matter between
The two of us.
It spends our very energy; that
We have conserved for
Each others use.

The grouping out of our
Thoughts is of no kind.
We must strengthen our forts of solidarity.
For as the sun shines,
I guided you, in a land of no sight.
Be I your eyes,
	Even in the morning
		Light.

Sling back your flightless wings
    Those with programmed speech
    Of razor sharp sounds
    Like hisses from a snake's den.

Throw back your youth forever.
    Or live Now.

Fly with determination of a not-earthly bird.
Be a fast-raving, fiendish pace-setter of true beauty
    As only a flower
    of your carriage needs no sun to grow
    but much sweetened water.

Water that comes only from knowing
    The rain itself.

Shower me in bliss of faith
    Or pour me down a downpour
Of blazing sun rays
    As a desert lives
        By sun of no worth.

And then
    The dawning of
      Reality –

Slowly, as the smoke
    clears and all
      can once again be seen;

You doubt in your treasure
    In knowing that though
      you'll never turn
        your back again,
It just won't be
    the same.

I touch you, I see and
Breathe you into my soul
I hold you, need
    you
        want you
But lo and behold—
There is something
    stronger
Much bolder and more
        meaningful

More meaningful than you
    A vibrant flow of life
        Yes—even you—
At its pace, even a top to spin twice
    before the glass turns to ice.

On the 7th I woke
Up with the knowledge.

The way I hear it
A Puerto Rican loves you more
Or hates you more.
Goes for broke
Every time the deck is dealt.

So, if you only cut the
Ice once, be sure it ain't
                    Glass.

030272 — Solitary Confinement

Slowly time erases faces from my mind.
No longer can faces agree with names
It's a big masquerade; time is!
It rips people from my grasp
          Throws them to the wind
Lingering before me this mountain foams.
It raves, it screams, it screeches, it rips through me.
          I am spent, lost and very much alone.
Time out from time !

Dear Anne,

       I received your letter today.

I was glad to know you are doing well, but a little upset to learn that the puppy died. I am well but a little lonely. Next time you right would you sort of let yourself go and wright " Love Anne"

                   Love always

                   Anthony Blade

                   759-35 42 – 01

                   Death Row Cell #6

Free wheelingly I grasp for no definite hold.
I clutch with open eyes in the dark, or better put
    Blindly into the light.
I am aware of all movements, except the movement
    of stillness.
I soar over the heads of would be people,
    slamming back my wings to prevent contact.
Nursing my broken down thoughts of laughter.
I denude my very mind so no trace will be found.
    Refusing to admit the blame for someone else's designs.
Dogs of caves smash against my very head and body.
Refusing to hand over a handful of names;
Knowing it to be my only way out,
I melt as the lasered words crush within my mind
As for the last time I smile.

Baby cries the Blues
   From first breath   t
               a
                  k
                     e
                        n
     for poor sweet Mama
     was way swayed into
                  a white river
     never ever thinking
     but of
     swimming to a
     tide
        not even she
        could
        swim against
        someway to know.

I will stay with you if your lights are out
I can function rather well
    In the dark.
I was in the dark a good part of my life
And when the light came on it hurt.
I saw things in the light that hurt my soul.
I agonized for knowing and accepting the fact that I was lost.
A lost man walking, map in hand, going nowhere fast.
Hell bent crazy and alone.

Locked up
                Locked in
        Locked out
Locked down
I found myself foolishly
        Trolling for trouble in 8 block A side
An argument jumped up and I was off
base. The Correctional Officer yelled all fucking right "A side on one
side B side on the other"

I used to walk in the darkest places. Where I walked was infested with no
Life of soul.
Things would break and people would fall away.
I lunge on my toe tips seeking to overcome all, just to leave that place
Alive.

1975–1985

But you realize,
That you can't go for her anytime
That you get to missing her;
Like you used to —
    For she ain't there now.

So instead, the time you feel you wish
To share, you pour it over
And pen your daytime evenings
    By mid-afternoons.

    What makes you so strong?

It sat there, perched;
Like a broke wing bird.
Waiting ————!
Around the mountain,
The second wind broke,
Giving it a full glide to
FLY ————!

While in another's company
I would see beautiful things.
And, rushing to you to let you
Know of these things I
Would not stop to really appreciate them.

Now you're gone.
We never saw these things
    Together.
But, no matter, I saw them
    for you.

oh street of poison
    where Babylon is true to work
as brother does in brother
stop selling yourselves to the vendors
of lusting hate or hateful lust.

Oh you lovely lady of cheer.
You set me aglow with no thought.
Just gazing and trying to out-stare
You, as you yourself like to stare.

You chose to tell me something
Pressing to mine—
You told me,
Something I would never forget.

The following meet you seemed to say
That you forgot what you had told me.

Why did you ask my
　　Work of devotion –
When all you did was
　　Step on it?

Come on Lady
Rain on me mama
Do what you need
But please,
Don't let me
drown.

As you go out of your self,
you'll turn left then right.
You are able to flex your judgment
So much before an actual bend – snaps.

You feel all is outcast in
origin as you spin off a cuff.
Only to retrieve your feelings of
a less point of demand.

Slowly I await the dolly
Hoping my need of solitude
Would weigh it down upon me
Causing it to rain and reek of
   My poisoned heart

What, you say she hasn't been by!
Well, I guess I will come by and by
Till I see her

If before your eyes
My past married my present,
Let us part
Lest we have no future.

Hell, it's six o'clock already!
Gotta get to work to start a day.
What was that zooming by?
A thought of yesterday's laughter,
A glimpse of tomorrow
And my death today.

You holler at not being
My first cup of tea.
I, who caffeine do not see
Yet and all I change my ways.
Only to have you spill my cup of tea.

I realized I didn't
Want to stop at the plant.
But to go on and on
Not caring of prison.

The sand drifts
with its coast.
The Sunrise 'gainst
The sunset
seems to boast.
Yet the true beauty
In life; I just learned
is a silent host.

Reach the top of the stairs
Go beyond
Look no more
As you
have now become part of your own.
Blow two lines
of trailing snow
from your path of illicit recruit.
Salvage together
that which belongs
to neither
Bring to pass the present
which wholly belongs
to a breeding mother of
blues-filled sanity
Go past
Go beyond
Go into yourself and see the beauty
You show me day in and day out
But! Go now or never see

I REMEMBER THE DAY
I BEGAN TO PRAY
PLEASE LET THAT LIGHT SKINNED
        GIRL
        LOOK MY WAY
        ALL HER FRECKLES BRING ME JOY
        SHE HAS BROWN
        SPANISH EYES
        I THINK SHE SEES ME
                IS SHE BEING COY?

just letting you know
how much I care.
When no one else was around
You were always there

I am a man of little words
I don't say much old or new
But the fact really is
That I am in love with you

come on lady
rain down on me
do what you need
but please
don't let me drown.

I've been running from time, yet all
By being here
I am looking at the face of a four-dollar watch,
which she by the way was to restore the face of.
It's as if a warm cold air
Lashes at my back
Cuffing at my ankles,
Tying me down to no ties.

Storming anger, known only by those
Who have amended today
To walk tomorrow

You are the dream iv wanted to realize
You are the rain on the mountain.
The sunset in the sky

You are so special
My heart beats out loud
The current in the ocean
the wind that pulls the cloud

So soft and so caring
you make me hear
the cry of a newborn
So watchful and so tentative
you are the eyes in my storm

the one I wish to grow old with
my morning darling dearest delight
the rhythm in my wellness
My sigh in the night

The Bell that tolls for me
the third graders glee
The apple in my eye
My honey Bea

Machinist by trade
Photographer by want
of freedom to express.

Willing always to test
The steps of a stair
     this stage takes me everywhere.

Steel toes to teeth.
And every low creature beneath
     that I trampled on, ran through
     or crawled beyond
As it bitingly poisoned me Blue.

I would like to put
    my lips to the heart of
      your breast
Where its field of hue
    is strawberry
      on crest.

14917

There came a time
When light came from darkness.
Truth has shone above all lies,
And from my weakness a
    Strength will arise –
I don't look to be as Sampson
    Nor as a fool –
I feel my strength in my foolish ways
    But I also feel an error
      In your days.

Oh you wonderful woman.
You stay in my mind
Like a token
At the station.

With pen and pad
I set out to examine
the true worth of our cross road affair.

At the beginning of our trek
it was you who waited.
Now, it is I.

I would tell you I'd be there
not to even show.
And you do the same from the word go.

I am now rude and crude
whereas before
I was at least well-mannered

Not even a full man am I now,
For, to you, I am a fool.
A whimpering child—gone wild.

Sometimes, you must do
Things you need to;
    To get where you are going.

Shade darkens even a minute.

Darkness blankets all,
Whereas light can only filter
Through the mush.

1985–2010

It's a feeling no one wants to have.
It's a pain we cry from before it even sets in.
It's the letting go of someone you didn't say goodbye to.
It's when they come to your door to tell you, a loved one is dead.
The pain, the tragedy, the grief, the drunk driver
    are all part of a man-made hell.

Then came the day
When all the skies
                    turned gray.
Thoughts were lost
With sorrows spoken
        of her true love
                    She bore fruit
                            a token.
She gave of herself
            to me a jewel
A bright pretty Pearl
My sun, My Girl.

When the stars fall
And there is no place
                    to go
The waters dry
            and the air is slow.

The heavens open
        the earth spins fast

My love for you will
                keep
                growing.

All this it will
            outlast.

A man does not know his own strength
Nor does he realize his own weakness.

I am going to kiss you
                    In the morning
I'll be kissing you this afternoon
                    as well
You need to know my darling
            Till you came along
                    I'd been living in hell.

Oh but a good wife
Is all a decent man needs?
Should she leave him or forsake him
He comes crashing to his knees

Going all the way to Jesus, so don't try to turn me round.

LET ME WRITE YOU
Though you won't allow me
The beauty of seeing you,
Then, at least look at me;
    Look inside.

Here, as you turn to your right,
You'll see a strength building.
And, as you turn towards your left,
You'll see what is left over
    From a time no more.

    Of brutal hate.
    Self disgust,
        And one nasty inner war.

I RAISE MY HAND
AND SAY, " I DO"
AND I DO PROMISE
TO LOVE ONLY YOU.
I KNOW THE REASON
    WHY WOMEN CRY
        BUT, I WILL BE WITH YOU TILL THE DAY I DIE
THOUGH YOU DON'T TRUST ME
YOU DOUBT.
        YET, I AM NOT KEEN ON STEPPING OUT.
EVERYTIME YOU LOOK
    I WILL BE RIGHT HERE
I WILL ALWAYS KNOW YOU
AS MY DARLING DEAR
    BE IT MORNING
        OR LATE AT NIGHT
YOU WILL FOREVER BE
    MY DARLING DEAREST DELIGHT.
    BECAUSE I LOVE YOU, BECAUSE I LOVE
        YOU YOU YOU

So much dull life that it seems
monkeys in cages in Brazil
are reaching through the fence openings
to make jest of us.

A BLIND SOUL
STUMBLES ON IN DARKNESS
VITAL KNOWLEDGE

What do you do
When you exhaust yourself
Body and soul
Trying to keep
The snake out
When all the time,
He is helping you lock
yourself away.

The most useful feeling
I've ever possessed
Is knowing you.

You save a lot of money
By not buying salt.

I ran away a drugged drunk fugitive
Came back a praying warrior

I knew it was now or never when I had
A minister in one room
And a crack dealer in the other.

I ran from my family knowing that
If I did not, my family would suffer
Drastically.
If crack were to take hold of me I knew I would die long before I
would ever leave this world.

I feel my Diablo/Saints were constantly at war within me.
I could not drag the mother of my children down like I had so many
people before her.
She made a difference, she was positive, sure of her self and way
better then me.

Iv been in numerous relationships so iv had my share of girlfriends,
that's all there is.
But of all of them, not one of them has ever fought for me the way
the mother
Of my children threw down for me
She on her own fought unknown to me, she fought against my
demons

I was not there for your first step
But I pray you will let me walk
You down the aisle

Can't recall when I first heard Daddy
But now it seems you've spruced it up
And I get to hear Daddio
Once in a while.

"When yesterday's become today."
and your horrid past runs into your present day and you
reap what you sowed.

I am at my crossroads
and i dont know what to do
My depression has me dealing
with my demons of loneliness
as I film a doc. about Sapphic Jews
Returning home.
I want their peace but yet the blows of friendship
send me deeper in to the hell I have come to know as
my life at my crossroads.

When the radio talks to him

He cries inside as he
    sings to the song they
            danced together –

Then he weeps to himself knowing he'll
        spend his hell alone

Cause when she went to heaven, he went to drinking
Cause he ain't been the same
        Not unless he hears their song
            PLACE called
            Heaven's Gate

I had a dreadful fall
It was my darkest day
I had been on the straight and narrow
And knowingly with intent, I took a left turn.

There were no banister or rail
To have kept me on path, simply the powerful love of something greater than I.
Yet I threw it all away. Now as I plummet down to my failure, I can only seek refuge,
within the face of grace.
Grasping out my stretched hands I reach for my beloved.
Praying to reach her door by the middle of night so I can awaken
to her face
and once again prepare for the battle of my darkest night.
I would that I place the amour complete upon my mind
so as to plunge into darkness yet find my path to being better
than who I was.

WHERE ARE ALL THE KIDS I USED TO PLAY WITH
WHERE ARE THE GANGS I USED TO FEAR
WHERE ARE ALL THE THINGS I USED TO RUN FROM
ALL WHILE STANDING HERE

TIME, IT HAS TAKEN AWAY ALL I KNEW
I AM STANDING ON THE CORNERS OF INTERVALE AND
KELLY
LOOKING STRIGHT DEAD AT YOU.
BUT YOU ARE NOT TO BE SEEN
NO ONE KNOWS WHO YOU ARE
YOU ARE NO LONGER THE MEAN KID
THE BRUTAL VENGEFUL CZAR

AND TO GOD I GIVE THE GLORY
FOR CHANGING YOU FROM WHO YOU ARE

SOMETIMES I CRY INTO THE STORM
AT BEST I CRINGE AT THE DARKNESS
THAT FALLS AS I SEARCH FOR THE LIGHT.

I KNOW THAT I AM NOT ALONE
I FEEL THAT AT TIMES
I AM MADE STRONG
BUT STILL I COWER BEFORE MY FIGHT.

I AM IN A CONSTANT BATTLE WITHIN MYSELF
DON'T BELIEVE ANY ONE CAN EVER LOVE ME
AS I AM.

I THRUST THE DAGGER IN MY OWN HEART
SO AS NOT TO HURT
MY LOVED ONES ANYMORE
I SIT, I CRY AT TIMES I DIE.

TO GET AWAY FROM ME, I CALL OUT NAMES
I DIAL THE PHONE, I EMAIL MYSELF AS I EAT
HUMBLE PIE

I SING, I RETREAT, I LAUGH AND SING
MAKING LIKE EVERYTHING IS FINE
YET IT IS WITH DEMONS
THAT I DINE
MY SKELETONS HAVE CLOSETD OF THEIR OWN.

I LONG FOR MY SOULMATE
WHOM I HAVE BURNED
I WANT MY CHILDREN
WHEN WILL I LEARN
IF I DON'T RETURN TO MY SANITY
MY LUCK WON'T TURN.
TODAY HAS BEEN ANOTHER
　　　HELL DAY FOR ME.
SO MUCH TO DO
SO MUCH TO SEE
BUT THERE IS NO ONE
TO SHARE IT WITH ME.

TATTOO YOU
I WANT THE SUN AND RAIN IN CAMPANA'S HAIR
I WENT FROM PRISON TATTOOS
TO LOVING YOU

BE I YOUR HEARTS CLOAK
   KEEPING YOU BRACED AND LOCKED
   IN THE WARMTH
   OF MY ETERNAL PASSION.
      I LIFT YOU TO MEANDER THRU THE STARS
      OF BLISS AS YOU PROPEL ME THRU
      THE GALAXY   WITH YOUR MADDENING
      SPANISH KISS
      OH THE LORD KNOWS THE THINGS I'V SEEN
      HE HAS BEEN IN THE MIDST OF ALL MY
      DREAMS.
      I FALL DOWN AND GET BACK UP WITH
      BRUISED KNEES
            AND BROKEN HEART
         KNOWING NOT WHERE TO GO
           OR HOW TO START

She truly is an anointed vessel
She is not only my life's partner
She is my companion in spirit
And my true best friend.

She is a warrior for God
Sent to gather the masses.
To prepare them for their journey home.

She is above all, a daughter of my God
She is a princess to my King.

She reaches into the depths of my hell
Burning herself going in and coming out
Yet, clutching on to me, yanking me from
my depression, as the Devil beats on her
With no mercy.

As my screaming agony rings out
Like three dead dogs that bark in the night
Yet, in her pain she screams to give me life
She brings me joy. She is my help meet. She is my wife.

Just letting you know
How much I care
When no one else was around
You were always there.

I am a man of little words
I don't say much old or new
But the fact really is
That I do love you.

I KNOW IN MY SOUL SHE IS DOWN
TO EARTH
FROM HER VERY FIRST KISS
I KNEW HER TO BE INTOXICATING.
I'V FOUND SOMEONE WHO IS STRONG
    AT PEACE WITH HERSELF
SOMEONE BETTER THAN ME
SOMEONE WHO KNOWS THE WORST SIDE OF ME
YET STILL LOVES ME.

I huffed
and I puffed
and I blew
my house down

I'm going to kill that
　　　Monster.
I'm going to take on that
One-eyed killer.

　　　And you shall be
　　　　the rock
　　　　　in my sling

Let her be my wife my Lord
Let her sing you praises
As we walk hand in hand

Even though I know my Lord
It was my name you wrote
In the sand.

I AM DEEP IN THE THROES OF DEPRESSION
I DON'T LOOK PEOPLE IN THE EYE
    FOR IF I DO
        THEY WOULD SEE
        AND I WOULD SURELY DIE.
WITH LAUGHING FACE
    I DANCE WITH GRACE
    I SMILE, I LAUGH, I SING
TWISTING AWAY THE PAIN
I PULL DOWN MY SLEEVES
    TO COVER UP THE TRACKS IN VAIN
    SO NO ONE CAN SEE THE BEGINNING OF
    MY END.
I AM IN A ROOM FULL OF PEOPLE
    YET STANDING ALONE IN MY HELL
I DON'T HAVE NO COMPANY
I DON'T HEAR MY BELL
    THE ONE THAT RUNG THAT I WAS FREE
    THE ONE, WHICH WITH A CLANG
        DARED ME TO BE.
AS I TURN THE KEY IN MY DOOR
    AND SO QUIETLY SLIP IN SIDE THE HOUSE
I START TO TREMBLE CAUSE NOW
IN THE DARK I SEE
    5 HUGE, CHAMPION DEMONS
    REACHING UP   TAKING HOLD
        OF ME
MY LORD MY LORD I TURN TO THEE

2010–2015

Do you think that there comes a time when
you stop feeling bad about being left
out of everything?

Cause I see no end!

Maybe I am done with being sober.

YOU ARE CAUGHT UP IN THIS DARKNESS
    ONLY YOU AND THE DEVIL UNDERSTAND
WHY A MAN WOULD CHOOSE TO RUN THIS PATH
    KNOWING IT TO BE QUICKSAND
I AM TRYING TO SHAKE THIS DARKNESS
    I'V ALREADY LOST MY SIGHT
CAUGHT UP BETWEEN TWO WORLDS
    IN ONE MEAN AWFUL NASTY FIGHT
I AM FIGHTING FOR MY LIFE SWEET JESUS
ONLY YOU CAN PULL ME OUT
THIS BATTLE WITH DEPRESSION
IS NOT MY FIRST BOUT.

I'V NEVER WASTED MORE TIME
    THAN THE VERY MINUTES I SPEND AWAY
    FROM YOU.
  SOME PEOPLE HEAD FOR THE MOUNTAINS
    OTHERS GO TO THE SHORE
    SOME LIKE TO GO CAMPING
      YET MANY OTHERS STAY INDOORS.
BUT, I KNOW BEST WHERE MY HEART
NEED TRAVEL
      WHEN THE WORLD IS IN GREAT ALARM
I KNOW WHERE PEACE GLADDENS MY SOUL
      MY LOVE AND BLISS I FIND IN YOUR ARMS.

OH
    I'VE NEVER PLAYED CATCH WITH MY FATHER
NEVER JOINED THE SCOUTS
               NOR THE PONY LEAGUE
NEVER REALLY HAD ANY FRIENDS AT ALL
               AT THE AGE OF NINE
HAD MY BACK TO THE WALL
    NEW YORK CITY BORN AND BRED
WARM GUN IN MY ARM
        COLD GUN TO YOUR HEAD.
GRADUATED FROM   PS 99,
               THE SCHOOL OF BROKEN DREAMS
BY THE FOLLOWING SUMMER, I WAS DOING JUVI TIME
               AND I WASN'T EVEN A TEEN.
               FIRST NIGHT IN THE REFORM
HAD TO PUT ON THE GLOVES
        WITH THE 3 BIGGEST CATS IN THE DORM
DIDN'T REALLY GIVE A CRAP
        TO ME THAT WAS THE NORM.
        I BEAT ALL 3, AS I WAS DOING TIME
WENT TO BOBING AND WEAVING
        WHILE I WAS GETTING MY RYHME.
YOU SEE, I HAD LEARNED TO FIGHT
        IN THE BOWELS OF HELL
EVERY FIGHT EVER FOUGHT IN MY SCHOOL YARD
HAD TO BE FOUGHT AND WON
        BEFORE THE RINGING OF THE LUNCH BELL.

What is it one must do
      to lock the snake out
Run to the front door
      to nail it shut
Reaching behind you
      Only to find the devil himself
handing you the nails from the cross

I am going to take life
    And hold it in place.

I've led such a fast life
that when I die
my heart will have to beat
inside someone else
for yet another life time
in order for me to find peace
within my soul

The mind I know
　　Is not to grow
In fiendish ways
　　Of destitute
Of hate and gore
Nor rendezvous with the enemy
　　　I write away my bad moments
I cry away my pain
　　　As I swiftly kill all presence
Of friendships
　　Sought in vain
I walk alone within myself

When Jesus Weeps
He weeps for me
As I hand up the 3rd nail
Feeling like I will never be free

He looks over thru misty eyes
to stare right at me

As He turns away moaning
not you, no not you
the mallet stakes his feet

in His agony He looks at me
In pain He whispers
   Let me count the ways that
     I love thee

When friends conspire to help someone they love
Take me up outside this earth
That I may ride with thee in the cover of the wind

I want to talk about a God who gives second chances.
He gave me a second chance.

Eres la maldicion de mis pecados

What it is to be blind.
I feel we live in darkness when we can not see who we really are

Sin Sick Soul
Didn't know who I was till
She walked into my heart.

I want you to be my wife.
You are my best of friends
Even with you not liking me
You are still the best in my life.

Yes you did
You changed my life
I would rather walk off the roof
Than not have you in my life

Your leaving taught me about true sorrow
but more so what real love is

I stay miserable
I haven't had slept
In a really long time
But iv learned to handle for you
I want to make right
I want to forget how to tie my shoes
I don't want to know how to spell me
I want to live codependent with you
I want to lose a part of me
To be with you.

Oh Lord I wonder why I feel like dying
Then I realize I am already
walking with the dead
Sometimes I feel like taking flight from this building
or simply put
Putting one through my head.
Iv never been so mother fucking alone.

I'v always felt the saddest any father
Could be was to die unsaved
To suffer in hell
And as lower level demons chewed
at his ankles, his head would turn
at the sound of a familiar voice:
"Dad I followed you here"

But seems Iv gone one better
My wife and I built new from
the ground up, a two story house.
My children were so happy and
my wife did all she could to make
this our first home. The problem is
When I walked in, I brought hell
with me, and for years my demons
tormented my family within our home.
My skeletons have closets of their own.

I want to go back to
Drinking cold beer
And making love to you
till 3 in the morning
And showing up for work
At six

I recall that making love to you
Was like holding onto a storm
and not being able to let go
till it passed
I miss the love you rained on me.
Would that I should walk with you
Again within a spring shower of bliss
At lightning speed I would kiss
the thunder from your heart
She's my honey
And my bunny
My sexy little dove
My sweetie and my lover
favor sent from up above
I am her New York second
and she is my Country Mile

Be i your hearts cloak
Keeping you braced and
Locked in the warmth of my
Eternal passion.

I lift you to meander thru the stars
of bliss as you propel me thru
The galaxy with your maddening
Spanish kiss

Oh the lord knows the things iv seen
He has been in the midst of all my dreams

The souls of your young people are stolen from you by drugs

I fall down I get back up with bruised knees and broken heart.
Knowing not where to go
or how to start

53012

My tribute
White flowers
White balloons
No friends
Just family
Drifters music
Only people that loved me can be invited.
Only C&C will open or close the front door to let people in

Need all grandchildren to be hugged
For me
Me viejo san juan

No vas a volver

I am glad God came and took me out to the woodshed.
My entire world collapsed around me.
I was getting too comfortable in hell.

It is because of grace
that I move thru this place
Blessed and highly favored.

IT'S SO SAD
    WHEN YOUR ATTITUDE
    IS OLD
AND YOU NEVER KNOW NEW

YOU CRY YOURSELF TO SLEEP
    BECAUSE YOU FEEL YOU ARE SO BAD
    NOT EVEN GOD, WANTS YOU
YOUR ATTITUDE IS BAD
AND YES, NO ONE CARES FOR YOU

OH LORD I BESEECH YOU
STRETCH OUT MY WINGS
SO THAT I MIGHT FLY.
SHOWER ME IN YOUR WISDOM
AS I SOAR THE SKY.
TEACH ME TO BE HUMBLE
WASH ME IN YOUR LOVING GRACE.
LORD, KEEP ME PANTING
TILL I SEE YOUR LOVING FACE.
NOW IN YOUR PRESENCE LORD
I HAVE A FAVOR TO ASK
I PLACE FORTH THIS PETITION
THOUGH IT NOT BE A TASK
THAT IF: IN THIS TIME AND PLACE
ONLY 1 CAN BE WITH YOU
NOT 2
THEN LET ME GO
AND SET BELL BROOKS
ON THIS WONDER FILLED JOURNEY WITH YOU.
MAY HER BURDENS, SORROWS AND PAINS
NOT BE USED AGAINST HER AS A TOOL
MAY YOUR VICTORIOUS GUIDING GLORY
MAKE HER SMILE, AS IN HER HEART
YOU ALREADY RULE.
SOOTHE AND KEEP HER
IN YOUR LOVING ARMS
AND SHELTER HER WONDERFUL SPIRIT
AS MY PRAYERS BECOME MY ALMS
BLESS YOU GOD AND THANKS FOR HEARING MY PLEA
YOU KNOW WHATS BEST FOR HER
MUCH BETTER THAN ME.

I AM FIGHTING FOR MY LIFE
   SWEET JESUS
      IF YOU DON'T WANT TO LOSE ME
      YOU ARE GOING TO HAVE TO
HELP ME
I AM GOING DOWN ONE MORE TIME

     THIS STRIKE IS #3

I'V SAID THINGS THE DEVIL
   COULD NOT BEAR
I'V DONE THINGS TO MAKE
THE ANGELS STARE
I'V DONE THINGS TO MY SOUL
WITHOUT A CARE
AND NOW
TO ANSWER TO GOD
I DON'T EVEN DARE

Let me gaze into your Texas size
    Spanish eyes
And let me see the joy in your face
    As my peace settles in forever
In your loving arms, you grant me this grace
    As I cascade into a coma
Let me rest my head on your soft shoulder
    And you cradle me into the hereafter.
Let me pass
With your heart beat and the songs from
Your youth
As from your lips I receive the last warm
Sweet breath, of your loving kindness
Blowing on my face as you sing
    Cielito lindo.
    Once I've left this place, go on singing
As you lay me down with our farewell kiss.
Fix my clothing and
    Comb my hair
Before you call our daughters
    In the room
And let them know I am with Jesus now
    But,
That wonder-filled trip to heaven
    Started in your loving arms
    However, many years ago.
    Canta y no llores.

I woke up Alive.
I danced, I laughed and thought of You.
Oh God.
I now know what was missing in me.
It was not me who was missing. I was there, suffering.
So I know I was there.
It was You who held the clouds in one hand and my joy in the other.

Not knowing how to let go
Lord I am looking for
    the rain
    of the victors who get left behind
Send down a flood
    of her memories
To help me withstand all of time
For though she is not here
I can always say that once
All was fine and she was mine

52716

Growing up in the Bronx was all I can talk about
till 2016
In May of that year my daughters and I went on a lifetime of dreams.
When my coworkers asked
about our adventure,
I simply said it was
an answered prayer.

Though I had left the joint
Years ago, it was as if I were still a
prisoner. Till finally Jesus set me free.

16102

Eres mi Tesoro
        Y te adoro
Tue eres muy bella
Eres la persona en mi, que no conoci

Eres lo bueno,
    Lo Dulce

Tu en mi encuentras
        Lo major
    Y me doy pena
Y lloro porque
    Tambien
        Lo peor

You are my treasure
and I adore you
You are so beautiful
You're the person in me Iv never been able to see

You are the good
the sweet

In me you find
the best
Yet I feel pain
at times I cry
because you also find
the worst

Funny when you live outside yourself.
You can see no wrong in who you are or what you do.
Then you see a movie or hear a song or write a book
about something life changing.

You actually get a chance to catch yourself
Inside yourself
Before falling
outside yourself.

APPENDIX: Julio Fernando Velez, a Timeline

1949 Born Lincoln Hospital, Bronx County, New York
1954 Joined first gang on while living on Hoe Avenue
1955 Walked onto the PS 99 schoolyard: First day of school
1957 Formed and became president of a gang: "The White Warriors"
1958 His father moved the family to Asheboro, North Carolina
1959 Moved back to the Bronx; his father turned him in to the cops for having a zip gun
1962 Graduated from "The School of Broken Dreams," PS 99
1963 That summer, he was sent to a reformatory
1965 Released after time served
1966 Returned to North Carolina
1967 An English teacher suggested he should write a book about the hell he called home
1968 Graduated from Asheboro High School; moved back to NYC to work at the 5&10 on Southern Boulevard and walked into the world of drugs; returned to North Carolina
1969/'70 Interstate Flight to avoid prosecution; turned 21 and became a fugitive
1970 Arrested in NYC; sent to Rikers Island, the largest penitentiary in the world
1972 Extradited to North Carolina; while in court, the Attica Prison Riot erupted
1972 Excommunicated from the Catholic Church; became Bro. Julio X., 3rd Lieutenant of the FOI (Fruit of Islam, a paramilitary group) at the Maximum Security Prison of Elmira
1974 Did a Turn Around, and began doing time for crimes committed in North Carolina
1975 Released after time served
1985 Witnessed a miracle
1986 (July) Went to a concert to get stoned, but instead had a spiritual conversion experience
1987 Battled depression; tried to grow up, spiritually, morally, and emotionally
1988/'89 The battle continued
1990 Fell in love with his wife all over again
1990–2010 Was living the family dream, working on this book
2009 Was received back into the church, nearly 40 years after being excommunicated
2010 The bottom fell out: lower level demons and personal conflict abound
2015 Resumed work on projects of passion
2018 Finalized this volume of poetry, in hopes that it will make a difference in the lives of others

Background information about the author's next project:
An autobiographical film titled *The Me I Never Knew*

While many people can remember childhoods filled with hugs, kisses, and laughter, Tony's earliest memory is of a neighborhood gang; a gang he joined at the tender age of seven. In "The Me I Never Knew," Tony tells his heartbreaking story from the perspective of his childhood self; a child who lost his innocence, and nearly lost his soul.

The neighborhoods of the Bronx, New York, were not kind to Tony and his family. Gangs of youth in run-down buildings created the backdrop for Tony's childhood. The environment at PS99, or as he calls it, the School of Broken Dreams, did little to help children such as Tony rise above their circumstances. With no positive role models and few visible options for a life outside of his violent world, Tony embraced the culture that surrounded him. One fateful day, his grandfather's brother was shot and killed over a domino game, and Tony wasn't about to let that go. With a fiery anger in his heart and a homemade zip gun in his hand, nine-year-old Tony went out to shoot a nine-year-old rival gang member. But that's just the beginning of Tony's story.

Within three years, Tony had a juvenile record and was sent to a reformatory in upstate New York where he spent time with some of the roughest kids in the Empire State.

His experience in a juvenile reform home did little to alter the course of his life. On his first night in the general population, he successfully beat up the three biggest and toughest boys there, one after another. When Tony's sentence was up, he was not allowed to return home because the home to which he would have returned was no home at all. Among other dangers, his best friend had become both a drug dealer and a heroine addict, despite being only 13. Seeing what drugs had done to his loved ones, a well-intentioned

Tony swore he would never go down that road. And for just a little while, things began to look up.

In an effort to save his family, Tony's father moved them all to North Carolina. Tony attended high school and graduated in 1968. But instead of finding a straight and narrow path, an independent Tony returned to New York and found that his old life had been waiting for him—a life of drug addiction that would take him hostage for nearly 20 years.

At first Tony was still somewhat aware that he was playing with fire, and he fought his addiction by returning to his family's home in North Carolina to try to kick his habit. Unfortunately, he brought his lifestyle home with him; one night, he, a friend, and a gun found themselves in trouble with the law. Fleeing to New York to avoid prosecution, Tony became an interstate criminal and a wanted fugitive on the night of his 21st birthday.

The return to New York triggered the return of his drug habits. Armed, addicted, and on the run, Tony was no longer just playing with fire; he was engulfed in flames. It wasn't long before the NYPD caught up with him. After facing a police-issued revolver, he found himself facing a stay at Rikers Island Penitentiary, the largest prison in the world, followed by four years at a maximum-security prison in upstate New York.

In 1971, partway through his sentence in New York, he was extradited to North Carolina to face felony charges. Meanwhile, the New York prison system had to be entirely locked down due to the infamous Attica Prison Riots. Upon Tony's return to New York, he learned that two prisoners, transferred from Attica, had a "green light" on him—orders to kill. He had two contracts out on his life and was trapped in prison with nowhere to run. It was fight or die. The best option he could see was to get excommunicated from the Catholic Church, become a Muslim, and surround himself with an army for protection. For three years he was known only as Anthony X, 3rd Lieutenant of the FOI (Fruit of Islam, a paramilitary branch of the Nation of Islam). This may have kept him alive physically, but spiritually he was on a dark path.

After serving his time in New York for stabbing a man, Tony did a turn-around in North Carolina to work on his 15-year sentence at "The Wall," a prison in Raleigh. During his time in North Carolina he would continue to burn in his own personal hell, even after he was released. This had been Tony's life since he was a little boy; it was the only path he knew. But God was about to redirect that path.

That redirection came on July 26, 1986. He was headed to a concert with one goal in mind: to get stoned. However, instead of getting stoned, Tony got saved. Tony heard God calling to him that night, and before he could really understand what was happening in his heart, he was giving his life to Jesus. This turn-around forever changed his life. But it did not end his woes.

Tony's conversion forced him to face some ugly things in his life. He began to battle his addictions, but he also had to fight depression, guilt, thoughts of suicide, and all manner of demons. He had to face the truth that it was time to grow up and take responsibility for who he was and what would become of him. After nearly 30 years of being burned by violence and drugs, he began to fight that fire. And in the process, he learned something valuable about the God he now serves.

The Bible tells a story of three men who were thrown into a furnace as a death sentence; when the guards looked into the furnace, to their surprise they saw not three but four figures there— the three men, and the Angel of God. Tony says he can relate to this story. He'll tell you from experience that sometimes in life you are engulfed in flames. But when God doesn't pull you from the fire, He jumps right into the fire alongside you.

Tony emerged from the flames of his past, burned yet refined. Scarred, but renewed. Now this true story is coming to life in print because of the passion of a man with a noble dream. Tony's real name is Julio Velez, and his dream is to keep children today from facing a dismal future like the one he once faced. Velez is putting his story into print and hopes to eventually film it, too. He dreams of using this story and others like it to help children in gang-ridden slums learn to reach for a better life. Velez's goal is to build a youth center in San Antonio's west side where young people can feel safe, learn productive skills, and begin to see that a wonderful world is out there for them. He wants children who have been burned by life to learn how to rise from the ashes.

For more information about Mr. Velez's work to help underprivileged children, or to assist with this goal, please send inquiries via email to JulioFromPS99@yahoo.com.